CLB 3259
© 1993 CLB Publishing, Godalming, Surrey, England.
All rights reserved.
This 1993 edition published by Crescent Books,
distributed by Outlet Book Company, Inc, a Random House Company,
40 Engelhard Avenue, Avenel, New Jersey 07001.

Random House
New York • Toronto • London • Sydney • Auckland

Color separations by Advance Laser Graphic Arts, Hong Kong.
Printed and bound in Hong Kong
ISBN 0 517 08751 0

FISH & SEAFOOD COOKING

CRESCENT BOOKS
NEW YORK • AVENEL, NEW JERSEY

Contents

Introduction

Fish and seafood are among our most valuable natural assets. They are high in easily digestible protein, low in fat, offer endless variety and are quick and easy to cook. The popularity of fish and seafood has waned in the recent past due to its unjustified reputation for being difficult to prepare. Today, however, people acknowledge that although it needs a little preparation, this is mostly very straightforward and is well worth the effort. And, of course, if you don't want to put in any effort, the selection of ready-prepared fresh and frozen fish in the supermarket grows larger every year.

Better refrigeration techniques have meant more and more consumers can now enjoy varieties of fish and seafood that once would have been considered very exotic. And unusual fish, that would once have been impossible to find, are now regularly available at supermarkets. The most important thing to bear in mind when buying fish and seafood is freshness. Buy the freshest produce you possibly can and you will not go wrong. Find a source that has a very high turnover and examine the produce carefully before you buy it. If it is fish, it should not smell "fishy" as this means it is past its best. It should be moist, the flesh firm and the eyes bright. Seafood, too, should be firm, have a good color and look moist and fresh.

Cooking fish and seafood is much more simple than many people imagine and it has the added advantage of being quick to cook. The essential point to remember is never to overcook fish and seafood as it quickly loses its lovely tasty juiciness. The best way to treat it, therefore, is to combine it with ingredients and sauces that enhance, rather than mask, this fresh flavor. It is for this reason that stuffed fish dishes are so popular – all the flavor of the fish is to the fore with a little stuffing to add extra "bite." Mixing fish and seafood in chowders is also wonderful as a whole variety of flavors such as crab, shrimp and mussels can be blended with your own favorite flavorings to create a dish that is completely original!

The recipes in this book highlight some of the tastiest recipes for fish and seafood, whether for a simple lunch dish or a family meal, but they should also inspire the cook to experiment with the expanded range of fish and seafood now available.

MUSSEL SOUP

Shellfish contain a multitude of vitamins and minerals, especially vitamins A, E, D and K, and this soup is a delicious way of making sure you have a good supply of all of these.

SERVES 4

3 quarts fresh mussels
¼ cup butter
2 onions, peeled and finely chopped
2 cloves garlic, crushed
1¼ cups dry white wine
1¼ cups water
2 tbsps lemon juice
2 oz fresh white bread crumbs
2 tbsps parsley, freshly chopped
Salt and freshly ground black pepper

1. Scrub the mussels with a stiff brush and remove any barnacle shells or pieces of seaweed that are attached to them.

2. Tap each mussel sharply to make sure that it closes tightly.

3. Melt the butter in a large saucepan and gently fry the onions and garlic until they are soft, but not browned.

4. Add the mussels, wine, water and lemon juice to the pan, and bring to a boil. Season with salt and pepper, then cover and cook for approximately 10 minutes or until all the mussel shells have completely opened.

5. Discard any mussels which have not opened fully.

6. Strain the mussels through a colander and return the juices and stock to the saucepan. Put the mussels in a serving dish and keep warm.

7. Add the bread crumbs and the parsley to the mussel juices and bring them to the boil. Adjust the seasoning, and pour over the mussels. Serve immediately.

TIME Preparation takes 15 minutes, cooking takes approximately 20 minutes.

WATCHPOINT When cooking fresh mussels, great care must be taken to ensure that they are safe to eat. Discard any that do not shut tightly before cooking, or do not open after cooking.

HOT AND SOUR SEAFOOD SOUP

This interesting combination of flavors and ingredients makes a sophisticated beginning to an informal meal.

SERVES 4

3 dried Chinese mushrooms
1 tbsp vegetable oil
¾ cup shrimp, shelled and deveined
1 red chili, seeded and finely sliced
1 green chili, seeded and finely sliced
½ tsp lemon rind, cut into thin slivers
2 green onions, sliced
2½ cups fish stock
1 tbsp Worcestershire sauce
1 tbsp light soy sauce
2 oz whitefish fillets
1 cake of fresh bean curd, diced
1 tbsp lemon juice
1 tsp sesame seeds
Salt and pepper
1 tsp fresh coriander, finely chopped
    (optional)

1. Soak the mushrooms in enough hot water to cover for 20 minutes, or until completely reconstituted.

2. Heat the vegetable oil in a large wok or frying pan, and add the shrimp, chilies, lemon rind and green onions. Stir-fry quickly for 1 minute.

3. Add the stock, the Worcestershire sauce and the soy sauce. Bring this mixture to a boil, reduce the heat and simmer for 5 minutes. Season to taste.

4. Remove the hard stalks from the mushrooms and discard them. Slice the caps very finely.

5. Cut the whitefish fillets into small dice, and add them to the soup, together with the bean curd and Chinese mushrooms. Simmer for a further 5 minutes.

6. Stir in the lemon juice and sesame seeds. Adjust the seasoning and serve sprinkled with chopped fresh coriander leaves, if desired.

TIME Preparation takes about 20 minutes, cooking takes about 20 minutes.

COOK'S TIP If you cannot buy coriander use parsley instead.

CHILLED SHRIMP, AVOCADO AND CUCUMBER SOUP

Avocado and cucumber give this soup its pretty color.

SERVES 4

8 oz unpeeled shrimp
1 large ripe avocado
1 cucumber
1 small bunch dill
Juice of half a lemon
1¼ cups chicken stock
2½ cups plain yogurt
Salt and pepper

1. Peel all the shrimp, reserving the shells. Add shells to chicken stock and bring to a boil. Allow to simmer for about 15 minutes. Cool and strain.

2. Peel the avocado and cut it into pieces. Cut 8 thin slices from the cucumber and peel the rest. Remove seeds and chop the cucumber coarsely.

3. Put the avocado and cucumber into a food processor or blender and process until smooth. Add a squeeze of lemon juice, and pour on the cold chicken stock.

4. Reserve a sprig of dill for garnish, and add the rest to the mixture in the processor and blend again.

5. Add about 1½ cups of yogurt to the processor and blend until smooth. Add salt and pepper. Stir in the peeled shrimp by hand, reserving a few as garnish.

6. Chill the soup well. Serve in individual bowls, garnished with a spoonful of yogurt, a sprig of dill, and thinly sliced rounds of cucumber.

TIME Preparation takes 15 minutes, cooking takes 15 minutes.

CRABMEAT BALLS

*Delicious an appetizer or a cocktail snack, crabmeat balls can be made ahead,
then coated and fried at the last minute.*

SERVES 6-8

1 lb fresh or frozen crabmeat, chopped
    finely
4 slices white bread, crusts removed and
    made into crumbs
1 tbsp butter or margarine
1 tbsp flour
½ cub milk
½ red or green chili, seeded and finely
    chopped
1 green onion, finely chopped
1 tbsp chopped parsley
Salt
Flour
2 eggs, beaten
Dry bread crumbs
Oil for frying

1. Combine the crabmeat with the fresh
bread crumbs and set aside.

2. Melt the butter and add the flour off the
heat. Stir in the milk and return to moderate
heat. Bring to a boil, stirring constantly.

3. Stir the white sauce into the crabmeat
and bread crumbs, adding the chili, onion
and parsley. Season with salt to taste, cover
and allow to cool completely.

4. Shape the cold mixture into 1 inch balls
with floured hands.

5. Coat with beaten egg using a fork to turn
balls in the mixture or use a pastry brush to
coat with egg.

6. Coat with the dry bread crumbs.

7. Fry in oil in a deep frying pan, saucepan
or deep-fat fryer at 350°F until golden
brown and crisp, about 3 minutes per batch
of 6. Turn occasionally while frying.

8. Drain on paper towels and sprinkle
lightly with salt.

TIME Preparation takes about 40-50 minutes, including time for the mixture
to cool. A batch of 6 balls takes about 3 minutes to cook.

Mussels Marinière

Brittany and Normandy are famous for mussels and for cream and
so cooks combined the two in one perfect seafood dish.

SERVES 4

---

3 quarts mussels
1½ cups white wine
4 shallots, finely chopped
1 clove garlic, crushed
1 bouquet garni
½ cup heavy cream
3 tbsps butter, cut into small pieces
2 tbsps fresh parsley, finely chopped
Salt and pepper

---

1. Scrub the mussels well and remove the beards and any barnacles from the shells. Discard any mussels that have cracked shells and do not close when tapped. Put the mussels into a large bowl and soak in cold water for at least 1 hour. Meanwhile, chop the parsley very finely.

2. Bring the wine to the boil in a large saucepan and add the shallots, garlic and bouquet garni. Add the mussels, cover the pan and cook for 5 minutes. Shake the pan or stir the mussels around frequently until the shells open. Lift out the mussels into a large soup tureen or individual serving bowls. Discard any mussels that have not opened.

3. Reduce the cooking liquid by about half and strain into another saucepan. Add the cream and bring to the boil to thicken slightly. Beat in the butter, a few pieces at a time. Season to taste, add the parsley and pour the sauce over the mussels to serve.

TIME Preparation takes about 30 minutes, cooking takes about 15 minutes.

SERVING IDEAS Serve as a first course with French bread, or double the quantity of mussels to serve for a light main course.

FISH TEMPURA

This is a traditional Japanese dish, which can be served as an unusual appetizer.

SERVES 4

---

12 uncooked large shrimp

2 whitefish fillets, skinned and cut into
   2 ¾-inch strips

Small whole fish, e.g. smelt or whitebait

2 squid, cleaned and cut into 3-inch strips

2 tbsps all-purpose flour

1 egg yolk

½ cup iced water

1 cup all-purpose flour

Oil for frying

6 tbsps soy sauce

Juice and finely grated rind of 2 limes

4 tbsps dry sherry

1. Shell the shrimp, leaving the tails intact. Wash the fish and the squid and pat dry. Sprinkle them all with the 2 tbsps flour.

2. Make a batter by beating together the egg yolk and water. Sieve in the 1 cup of flour and mix in well with a knife.

3. Dip each piece of fish into the batter, shaking off any excess.

4. In a wok or deep-fat fryer, heat the oil to 350°F. Lower in the fish pieces a few at a time and cook for 2-3 minutes. Lift them out carefully and drain on paper towels, keeping warm until required.

5. Mix together the soy sauce, lime juice, rind and sherry and serve as a dip with the cooked fish.

TIME Preparation takes about 30 minutes, cooking time varies from 2 to 3 minutes depending on the type of fish.

VARIATIONS Use a few vegetables, as well as fish, for an interesting change. Whole mushrooms are especially good.

SALMON PÂTÉ

This highly nutritious, elegant pâté is low in fat and very quick to prepare.

SERVES 4

8 oz can red or pink salmon, drained
½ cup low fat cottage cheese
Few drops lemon juice
Pinch ground mace, or ground nutmeg
¼ tsp Tabasco sauce
Freshly ground sea salt and black pepper
2 tbsps low fat plain yogurt
4 small pickles

1. Remove any bones and skin from the salmon. In a bowl, work the fish into a smooth paste with the back of a spoon.

2. Beat the cottage cheese until it is smooth.

3. Add the salmon, lemon juice, seasonings, and yogurt to the cheese and mix well, until thoroughly incorporated.

4. Divide the mixture equally among 4 individual ramekins. Smooth the surfaces carefully.

5. Slice each pickle lengthways, 4 or 5 times, making sure that you do not cut completely through the pickle at the narrow end. Splay the cut ends into a fan, and use these to decorate the tops of the pâtés in the ramekins.

TIME Preparation takes about 15 minutes.

PREPARATION If you have a food processor or blender you can work the cheese and salmon together in this, instead of beating them in a bowl.

DRESSED CRAB

*No book on fish cookery would be complete without instructions on how to dress
a crab. Crabs should have rough shells, large claws and feel heavy for their size.
Do not buy a crab that sounds to have water in when shaken.*

SERVES 2-3

1 large cooked crab (see note)
Chopped fresh parsley, to garnish

1. Pull off the crab claws, and crack these
with a small hammer or nutcrackers. Pull
out the meat and put into a bowl for light
meat.

2. Turn the crab onto its back or uppermost
shell, and pull the underbody firmly away
from the main shell.

3. Remove and discard the stomach bag
and gray, feathered gills, or fingers, as these
must not be eaten. Scoop out the dark meat
from the shell with a spoon and put into a
bowl.

4. Crack open the underbody and remove
all the white meat with a skewer or fork. Put
into the appropriate bowl.

5. Remove enough of the top shell to make
a flat case, in which to serve the meat.
Scrub the shell thoroughly.

6. Arrange layers of dark and light meat
alternately in the shell, and garnish with the
parsley.

TIME Preparation takes about 35-45 minutes.

SERVING IDEAS Serve with new potatoes and a simple, mixed lettuce
salad.

PREPARATION To cook a hard-shell crab, place crab in a saucepan of
boiling, salted water, reduce heat and simmer for 20-25 minutes.

BROILED OYSTERS

Oysters are so delicious they need only simple treatment to be at their best.

SERVES 4

2 dozen oysters
¼ cup butter
1¼ cups heavy cream
1 small jar red caviar
Salt
Pepper
Tabasco

Garnish
Watercress

1. Open oysters and leave them in their half-shells (or buy them already opened).

2. Put a drop of Tabasco on each oyster, season, then add 1½ tsps of heavy cream.

3. Melt butter and sprinkle it over oysters. Put them under a broiler for 2-3 minutes.

4. When cooked, top each one with 1 tsp red caviar, and serve hot with bouquets of watercress as garnish.

TIME Preparation takes 10 minutes, cooking takes 2-3 minutes.

MATELOTE

A tasty, impressive dish perfect for entertaining.

SERVES 4

1 lb lemon sole
1 lb monkfish
1 small wing of skate
4 cups mussels
8 oz unpeeled shrimp
3 onions
⅓ cup butter
2 cups white wine
¼ cup flour
2 tbsps parsley, chopped
Salt
Freshly ground black pepper
Lemon juice

1. Fillet and skin the lemon sole. Cut the sole fillets and monkfish into large pieces. Chop the skate wing into 4 large pieces.

2. Peel the shrimp and set aside. Scrub the mussels well, discarding any with broken shells.

3. Chop the onion finely. Melt half the butter in a saucepan and soften the onion in a large saucepan.

4. Add the mussels and about 3-4 tbsps water. Cover the pan and shake over a high heat until all the mussels have opened, discarding any that have not.

5. Strain the liquid into a bowl, allow mussels to cool, and then shell them.

6. Return the cooking liquid to the saucepan. Place the pieces of fish in the liquid. Add the wine until it just covers the fish. Simmer gently for about 8 minutes or until fish is just cooked.

7. Mix together the flour and the remaining butter to make a paste.

8. Remove the cooked fish from the liquid and put into a serving dish to keep warm. Bring liquid to a boil. Add the flour and butter paste, a little at a time, whisking it in and allowing liquid to boil after each addition, until liquid is thickened.

9. Add the parsley, shelled shrimp, shelled mussels, a little lemon juice, and seasoning. Heat for a few minutes to warm the shellfish through. Pour over the fish in the serving dish and sprinkle with more chopped parsley if desired.

TIME Preparation takes 20 minutes, cooking takes 20 minutes.

MUSSELS ALLA GENOVESE

Mussels Italian style – the perfect start to any meal.

SERVES 4

3 lbs mussels
Juice of 1 lemon
1 shallot
1 handful fresh basil leaves, or 1 tsp dried
    basil
1 small bunch parsley
¼ cup walnut halves
1 clove garlic
2 tbsps freshly grated Parmesan cheese
3-6 tbsps olive oil
2 tbsps butter
Salt and pepper
Flour or oatmeal

Garnish
Fresh basil leaves

1. Scrub the mussels well and discard any with broken shells or those that do not close when tapped. Put the mussels into a bowl of clean water with a handful of flour or oatmeal. Leave for ½ hour, then rinse under clear water.

2. Chop the shallot finely and put into a large saucepan with lemon juice. Cook until shallot softens.

3. Add the mussels and a pinch of salt and pepper. Cover the pan and cook the mussels quickly, shaking the pan. When mussel shells have opened, take mussels out of the pan, set aside and keep warm. Discard any that do not open. Strain the cooking liquid for possible use later.

4. To prepare Genovese sauce, wash the basil leaves, if fresh, and parsley, peel the garlic clove and chop coarsely, and chop the walnuts coarsely.

5. Put the herbs, garlic, nuts, 1 tbsp grated cheese and salt and pepper into a food processor and work to chop coarsely. Add butter and work again. Turn machine on and add oil gradually through the feed tube. If the sauce is still too thick, add the reserved liquid from cooking the mussels.

6. Remove the top shells from mussels and discard. Arrange mussels evenly in 4 shallow dishes, spoon some of the sauce into each, and sprinkle the top lightly with remaining Parmesan cheese.

7. Garnish with basil leaves and serve.

TIME Preparation takes 15 minutes, cooking takes 5-8 minutes.

CRAB AND CITRUS SALAD

This delicious salad is perfect for a summer lunch.

SERVES 4

---

8 oz crabmeat, or 1 large crab

2 oranges

2 lemons

2 limes

1 pink grapefruit

1 small iceberg lettuce

½ cup plain yogurt

6 tbsps heavy cream

1 tbsp chili sauce

½ tbsp brandy

Pinch of cayenne pepper

Salt

2 tbsps salad oil

---

1. Separate the body from the shell of the whole crab, and remove and discard the lungs and stomach sac. Chop body into 3 or 4 pieces with a very sharp knife and pick out the meat. Scrape brown meat from inside shell and add to body meat.

2. Break off large claws and remove meat from legs; then crack the claws and remove claw meat.

3. Mix all the meat together and reserve legs for garnish. If using canned or frozen crabmeat, pick over the meat to remove any bits of shell or cartilage.

4. Mix together yogurt, chili sauce, cream, brandy, cayenne pepper and a pinch of salt, and toss with the crabmeat.

5. Take a thin strip of peel from each of the citrus fruits, scraping off the bitter white pith. Cut each strip of peel into thin slivers. Put into boiling water and allow to boil for about 1 minute. Drain, refresh under cold water, and set aside.

6. Peel each of the citrus fruits and cut into segments; do all this over a bowl to reserve juices.

7. Add 2 tbsps salad oil to the juice in the bowl, and toss with citrus segments. Shred iceberg lettuce and arrange on plates. Put the crabmeat in its dressing on top of lettuce.

8. Arrange citrus segments over and around crabmeat and sprinkle citrus peel over the top.

TIME Preparation takes about 20 minutes.

SOUR FRIED SEAFOOD

A fragrant sour fried curry from the Far East. This can be served on its own, or as one of a combination of dishes.

SERVES 4

1 lb mixed fish and seafood, to include any of the following: large shrimp; scallops; squid, cleaned and cut into rings; oysters, shelled; clams, shelled; crab claws, shelled; small whole fish, e.g. whitebait or smelt.

½ cup oil

1 tbsp fresh ginger, grated

4 shallots, finely chopped

3 cloves garlic, crushed

4 red chili peppers, seeded and finely chopped

1 tsp ground mace

½ tsp shrimp paste

1 piece tamarind, soaked in 4 tbsps hot water (see variation)

Pinch soft brown sugar

Salt

1. Heat the oil in a frying pan over a high heat. Fry the fish in several batches for 2-3 minutes per batch, or until lightly browned and cooked through. Drain on paper towels and keep warm.

2. Grind the shallots, ginger, garlic, chilies and mace to a smooth paste in a mortar and pestle. Add the shrimp paste and blend together well.

3. Put 1 tbsp of oil into a wok and add the spice paste. Cook gently for 2-3 minutes. Strain in the tamarind and water or lemon juice. The sauce should be of a thin coating consistency; add a little more water, if it is too thick.

4. Stir in the sugar, the cooked fish and salt to taste. Cook for 2-3 minutes, or until the fish is heated through.

TIME Preparation takes about 20 minutes, cooking takes about 12-15 minutes.

COOK'S TIP Great care should be taken when preparing fresh chilies. Always wash hands thoroughly afterwards, and avoid getting any neat juice in the eyes or mouth. Rinse with copious amounts of clear water if this happens.

VARIATION If tamarind is not available, substitute 2 tbsps of lemon juice.

MUSSELS À LA GRECQUE

Fresh mussels are a real treat during the fall and winter and the sauce in this recipe is a reminder of warmer days!

SERVES 4

4 cups mussels
1 onion, chopped
½ cup white wine
Juice of ½ lemon
2 tbsps olive oil
1 clove garlic, crushed
1 shallot or 2 green onions, chopped
1½ lbs fresh tomatoes, chopped
1 tsp fennel seeds
1 tsp coriander seeds
1 tsp crushed oregano
1 bay leaf
1 tbsp fresh basil, chopped, or ½ tsp dried
Pinch cayenne pepper
Salt and pepper
Black olives, to garnish

1. Scrub the mussels and discard any with broken shells, or which do not shut when tapped with a knife.

2. Put them into a large saucepan with the onion, wine and lemon juice. Cover and cook quickly for about 5 minutes until the mussels open, discarding any that do not.

3. Remove the mussels from their shells and leave to cool. Reserve the cooking liquid.

4. Heat the olive oil in a saucepan and add the garlic and the shallot or green onions. Cook gently, until golden brown.

5. Stir in the tomatoes, spices and herbs. Season to taste and blend in the reserved liquid from the mussels. Bring this mixture to a boil and allow to boil rapidly, until the tomatoes are soft and the liquid is reduced by half. Remove the bay leaf.

6. Allow the sauce to cool, then stir in the mussels. Chill well and serve garnished with black olives.

TIME Preparation takes about 20 minutes, including cleaning the mussels. Cooking takes about 20 minutes.

SERVING IDEAS Serve with a green salad and French bread.

SHRIMP PASTRY PUFFS

These light pastry puffs are excellent savory snacks for a picnic or informal party.

SERVES 4

---

6 tbsps butter

⅓ cup water

Generous ¾ cup all-purpose flour, sifted

3 eggs, beaten

3 tbsps butter

6 tbsps flour

1¼ cups milk

2 tbsps white wine

1 bay leaf

1 cup peeled shrimp, chopped

2 hard-cooked eggs, chopped

Pinch nutmeg

1 tsp fresh dill or ½ tsp dried, chopped

Salt and pepper

---

1. Put the 6 tbsps butter and the water into a saucepan. Bring to a boil. Tip in the ¾ cup flour all at once and beat until the mixture is smooth and leaves the sides of the pan clean. Leave to cool slightly.

2. Add the beaten eggs gradually to the flour mixture, beating vigorously, until they are well incorporated and the mixture forms a smooth, shiny paste.

3. Line a cookie sheet with wax paper and drop heaped teaspoonsful of the mixture onto it, spaced well apart. Bake in a preheated oven, 400°F, for 25 minutes, or until the pastry puffs are firm to the touch and golden brown.

4. Melt the remaining butter in a saucepan and stir in the remaining flour. Blend in the milk gradually, beating well between additions. When all the milk is mixed in, add the wine and bay leaf and bring to a boil, stirring constantly.

5. Remove the bay leaf, reduce heat and stir in the remaining ingredients. Heat for 2-3 minutes more.

6. Cut the pastry puffs almost in half through the middle and fill with the shrimp and egg mixture.

TIME Preparation will take about 15 minutes, cooking takes about 30-35 minutes.

COOK'S TIP To make sure that the pastry puffs stay crisp, after baking is complete, make a small slit in the side of each puff and return them to the oven, with the heat switched off, for 5 minutes, so that they dry out completely.

SALMON AND VEGETABLE SALAD

The fish in this salad "cooks" in the refrigerator in its vinegar marinade. Insist on very fresh fish for this recipe.

SERVES 4

12 oz salmon fillets
2 carrots, peeled and diced
1 large zucchini, peeled and diced
1 large turnip, peeled and diced
Chopped fresh coriander or pinch of dried
3 tbsps tarragon or wine vinegar
Salt and pepper
Pinch cayenne pepper
3 tbsps olive oil
Whole coriander leaves to garnish

1. Skin the salmon fillet and cut the fish into 1 inch pieces. Place in a bowl and add the vinegar, stirring well. Leave to stand for at least 2 hours.

2. Cut the vegetables into ½ inch dice and place the carrots in a saucepan of boiling water for about 5 minutes. Add the zucchini and turnip during the last minute of cooking time. Drain well.

3. Add the coriander, oil, salt and pepper and pinch cayenne pepper to the fish. Combine with the vegetables, mixing carefully so the fish does not break up. Chill briefly before serving and garnish with fresh coriander if available.

TIME Preparation takes about 30 minutes, with 2 hours for the salmon to marinate.

COOK'S TIP Fish allowed to marinate in vinegar, lemon or lime juice will appear opaque and "cooked" after standing for about 2 hours.

FISHERMAN'S STEW

*This quick, economical and satisfying fish dish will please any fish lover for
lunch or a light supper.*

SERVES 4-6

6 tbsps olive oil
2 large onions, sliced
1 red pepper, seeded and sliced
1½ cups mushrooms, sliced
16oz can tomatoes
Pinch salt and pepper
Pinch dried thyme
1¾ cups water
2 lbs cod or other whitefish fillets, skinned
¾ cup white wine
2 tbsps parsley, chopped

1. Heat the oil in a large saucepan and add the onions. Cook until beginning to look transluscent. Add the red pepper and cook until the vegetables are softened.

2. Add the mushrooms and the tomatoes and bring the mixture to a boil.

3. Add thyme, salt, pepper and water and simmer for about 30 minutes.

4. Add the fish and wine and cook until the fish flakes easily, about 15 minutes. Stir in parsley.

5. To serve, place a piece of toasted French bread in the bottom of the soup bowl and spoon over the fish stew.

TIME Preparation takes about 20 minutes, cooking takes about 45 minutes.

VARIATIONS Shellfish may be added with the fish, if desired. Substitute green peppers for red peppers.

SERVING IDEAS The stew may also be served over rice. Accompany with a green salad.

SALADE NIÇOISE

This classic French salad is a meal in itself when served with a green salad and some crusty bread.

SERVES 4

---

2 large, or 6 small, new potatoes, cooked and cut into ½ inch dice

6 oz green beans, trimmed and cooked

3 oz black olives, halved and stoned

1 small cucumber, diced

4 tomatoes, cut into eight

6 oz can tuna, in water

¾ cup peeled shrimp

4 hard-cooked eggs, shelled and quartered lengthwise

2 oz can anchovies, drained and chopped

6 tbsps olive oil

2 tbsps white wine vinegar

3 tbsps chopped fresh mixed herbs or 1 tbsp dried

2 tsps Dijon mustard

Salt and pepper

1. In a large bowl, mix together the potatoes, beans, olives, cucumber and tomatoes.

2. Drain the tuna and flake it with a fork. Mix this, along with the shrimp, eggs and anchovies into the salad mixture.

3. In a small bowl, mix together the oil, vinegar, herbs and mustard. Whisk with a fork until thick.

4. Pour the dressing over the salad ingredients and stir gently to coat evenly. Season to taste.

TIME Preparation takes about 20 minutes, cooking takes about 20 minutes.

PREPARATION If you have a screw top jar, the dressing ingredients can be put into this and shaken vigorously, until they have thickened.

COOK'S TIP The dressing used in this recipe is delicious and will keep for up to 2 weeks in a refrigerator. So make double quantities and keep some to enliven other salad meals.

VARIATION If fresh herbs are not available substitute 1 tbsp dried mixed herbs.

Coconut Fried Fish with Chilies

A real treat for lovers of spicy food.

SERVES 4

Oil for frying
1 lb sole or other white fish fillets, skinned,
    boned and cut into 1 inch strips
Seasoned flour
1 egg, beaten
¾ cup shredded coconut
1 tbsp vegetable oil
1 tsp fresh ginger, grated
¼ tsp chili powder
1 red chili, seeded and finely chopped
1 tsp ground coriander
½ tsp ground nutmeg
1 clove garlic, crushed
2 tbsps tomato paste
2 tbsps tomato chutney
2 tbsps dark soy sauce
2 tbsps lemon juice
2 tbsps water
1 tsp light brown sugar
Salt and pepper

1. In a frying pan, heat about 2 inches of oil to 375°F. Toss the fish strips in the seasoned flour and then dip them into the beaten egg. Roll them in the shredded coconut and shake off the excess.

2. Fry the fish, a few pieces at a time, in the hot oil and drain them on paper towels. Keep warm.

3. Heat the 1 tbsp oil in a wok or frying pan and fry the ginger, red chili, spices and garlic, for about 2 minutes.

4. Add the remaining ingredients and simmer for about 3 minutes. Serve the fish, with the sauce served separately.

TIME Preparation takes about 30 minutes, cooking takes about 30 minutes.

SERVING IDEAS Serve with plain boiled rice, a cucumber relish and plenty of salad.

SWORDFISH KEBABS

Swordfish won't fall apart during cooking – a bonus when making kebabs.

SERVES 4-6

2¼ lbs swordfish steaks
6 tbsps olive oil
1 tsp chopped fresh oregano or ½ tsp dried
1 tsp chopped fresh marjoram or ½ tsp dried
Juice and rind of ½ lemon
4 tomatoes, cut in thick slices, or cherry tomatoes
2 lemons, cut in thin slices
Salt and freshly ground pepper
Lemon slices and Italian flat leaf parsley for garnish

1. Cut the swordfish steaks into 2 inch pieces.

2. Mix the olive oil, herbs, lemon juice and rind, and seasoning together and set it aside. Thread the swordfish, tomato slices or cherry tomatoes and lemon slices on skewers, alternating the ingredients. Brush the skewers with the oil and lemon juice mixture and cook under a preheated broiler for about 10 minutes, basting frequently with the lemon and oil. Serve garnished with lemons and parsley.

TIME Preparation takes about 15 minutes, cooking takes about 10 minutes.

VARIATIONS Fresh tuna may be used instead of swordfish.

SERVING IDEAS Accompany the kebabs with risotto and a green salad.

FRIED FISH WITH GARLIC SAUCE

Fish in such an attractive shape makes an excellent snack.

SERVES 4

2 lbs fresh anchovies or whitebait
1 cup all-purpose flour
4-6 tbsps cold water
Pinch salt
Oil for frying

Garlic Sauce

4 slices white bread, crusts trimmed, soaked
    in water for 10 minutes
4 cloves garlic, peeled and coarsely
    chopped
2 tbsps lemon juice
4-5 tbsps olive oil
1-2 tbsps water (optional)
Salt and pepper
2 tsps fresh parsley, chopped
Lemon wedges for garnishing (optional)

1. Sift the flour into a deep bowl with a pinch of salt. Gradually stir in the water in the amount needed to make a very thick batter.

2. Heat enough oil for frying in a large, deep pan. A deep-sided frying pan is ideal.

3. Take 3 fish at a time and dip them into the batter together. Press their tails together firmly to make a fan shape.

4. Lower them carefully into the oil. Fry in several batches for 3-4 minutes until crisp and golden. Continue in the same way with all the remaining fish.

5. Meanwhile, squeeze out the bread and place in a food processor or blender with the garlic and lemon juice. With the processor or blender running, add the oil in a thin, steady stream. Add water if the mixture is too thick and dry. Add salt and pepper and stir in the parsley by hand. When all the fish are cooked, sprinkle lightly with salt and serve with the garlic sauce and lemon wedges, if desired.

TIME Preparation takes about 30 minutes, cooking takes about 3 minutes per batch for the fish.

PREPARATION Coat the fish in the batter just before ready for frying.

VARIATIONS Fish may be dipped in the batter and fried singly if desired. Other fish, such as smelt or sardines, may also be used. Use thin strips of cod or halibut as well. Vary the amount of garlic in the sauce to your own taste.

VINEGARED CRAB

An unusual way of serving fresh crab. You should be able to buy the rice vinegar from a supermarket or health food store. If not, substitute white wine vinegar.

SERVES 4

1 cucumber, grated

Salt, for sprinkling

1 large cooked crab

1 small piece fresh ginger, grated

Chinese cabbage, for serving

3 tbsps rice vinegar

2 tbsps dry sherry

2 tbsps soy sauce

1. Sprinkle the cucumber with salt and leave for 30 minutes.

2. Crack the legs and claws off the crab. Remove the meat from the claws and legs, but leave four thin legs whole as a garnish.

3. Separate the underbody from the shell. Remove and discard the stomach sac and the gray, feathered gills.

4. Scrape the brown meat from the shell and crack open the underbody. Use a skewer to pick out the meat.

5. Rinse the cucumber, drain well and squeeze out excess moisture. Mix together the cucumber, crab meat and ginger.

6. Arrange the Chinese cabbage on serving plates, to represent crab shells. Pile equal quantities of crab mixture onto the Chinese cabbage, leaving some of the leaf showing. Garnish with a whole crab leg and some grated, pickled ginger, if you can get it.

7. Mix together the vinegar, sherry and soy sauce. Serve in little bowls with the crab.

TIME Preparation takes about 30 minutes.

SERVING IDEAS A rice or pasta salad would be excellent with this dish.

SHRIMP AND CASHEWS IN PINEAPPLE WITH TARRAGON DRESSING

Served in the pineapple shells, this impressive salad is ideal for a summer lunch.

SERVES 4

2 small fresh pineapples, with green tops
1¼ cups cooked, peeled shrimp
1 cup roasted, unsalted cashew nuts
2 celery stalks, thinly sliced
4 tbsps lemon juice
1 egg
2 tbsps superfine sugar
1 tbsp tarragon vinegar
2 tsps chopped fresh tarragon or 1 tsp dried
½ cup heavy cream

1. Cut the pineapples carefully in half lengthwise, leaving their green tops attached.

2. Cut out the pineapple flesh carefully, leaving a ¼ inch border of flesh on the inside of the shell. Remove the cores and cut the flesh into bite-sized pieces.

3. Put the chopped pineapple into a bowl, along with the shrimp, cashew nuts and celery. Pour in the lemon juice and mix well. Divide the mixture equally between the pineapple shells, and chill them in the refrigerator.

4. In a heat-proof bowl, whisk together the egg and sugar. Stand the bowl over a pan of simmering water, and whisk in the vinegar and tarragon. Continue whisking until the mixture has thickened.

5. Remove the bowl from the heat and allow to cool completely, whisking occasionally.

6. When completely cold, whip the cream until it is just beginning to thicken, then fold it into the dressing mixture.

7. Pour the cream dressing over the salad in the pineapple shells and serve.

TIME Preparation takes about 30 minutes, cooking takes about 10-15 minutes.

Spanish Rice and Sole Salad

A complete meal in itself, this salad is ideal for a summer lunch.

SERVES 4

2 large lemon sole, each filleted into 4 pieces

4-6 peppercorns

Slice of onion

1 tbsp lemon juice

¾ cup long grain rice

1 small eggplant

2 tbsps olive oil

1 red pepper, seeded and chopped into ¼ inch dice

1 shallot, finely chopped

1 green pepper, seeded and chopped into ¼ inch dice

3 tbsps Italian dressing

1 tbsp chopped fresh mixed herbs or ½ tsp dried

1 cup mayonnaise

1 clove garlic, crushed

1 tsp tomato paste

1 tsp paprika

Salt and pepper

2 bunches watercress, to garnish

1. Lay the sole fillets in an ovenproof dish, together with the peppercorns, slice of onion, lemon juice and just enough water to cover. Sprinkle with a little salt and cover the dish with foil or a lid. Poach in a preheated oven, 350°F, for 8-10 minutes. Allow the fish to cool in the liquid, then cut each fillet into 1 inch pieces.

2. Cook the rice in boiling water until soft. Rinse in cold water and separate the grains with a fork.

3. Cut the eggplant in half and sprinkle with 2 tsps salt. Allow to stand for half an hour, then rinse very thoroughly. Pat dry and cut into ½ inch dice.

4. Heat the oil in a large frying pan, and fry the eggplant, until it is soft. Allow the eggplant to cool, then mix it into the rice along with the shallot, peppers, half the chopped herbs and the Italian dressing.

5. Mix together the mayonnaise, garlic, tomato paste, paprika, remaining herbs and seasoning.

6. Arrange the rice on one side of a serving dish and the sole pieces on the other. Spoon the mayonnaise over the sole and garnish the dish with watercress.

TIME Preparation will take about 20 minutes, cooking takes about 15-20 minutes.

SOLE AND MUSHROOM TURNOVERS

These delicious individual pies make a warming family lunch or supper dish.

SERVES 4

4 sole fillets, skinned
Salt and pepper
½ cup milk
1 cup mushrooms, trimmed and thinly
    sliced
2 tbsps butter
Juice of 1 lemon
5 tbsps white bread crumbs mixed with
    1 tbsp crushed hazelnuts
3 tbsps hazelnut, or lemon stuffing mix
12 oz puff pastry
Beaten egg, for glazing
Poppy seeds, for sprinkling

1. Season the sole fillets and roll them up jelly roll fashion. Secure each roll with a wooden pick and poach gently in the milk for about 10 minutes in a preheated oven, 350°F.

2. Drain the fish and allow it to cool. Remove the wooden picks.

3. Put the mushrooms and butter in a saucepan with the lemon juice. Cook over a moderate heat for about 5 minutes.

4. Allow the mushrooms to cool and then stir in the bread crumb mix.

5. Roll out the pastry, quite thinly, into 4 circles, each 6 inches in diameter. Brush the edges with beaten egg.

6. Put a fish roll into the center of each circle and top with a quarter of the mushroom mixture. Pull the pastry edges up and over the fish and pinch together to seal.

7. Preheat the oven to 400°F. Place the turnovers on a greased cookie sheet and glaze with the beaten egg. Sprinkle with a few poppy seeds.

8. Bake in the pre-heated oven for about 25 minutes, or until well risen, puffed and golden. Serve piping hot.

TIME Preparation will take about 25 minutes, plus the cooling time, cooking will take about 35 minutes.

FISH, ZUCCHINI AND LEMON KEBABS

Buy the fish ready filleted and skinned, if you feel that you cannot do it yourself.

SERVES 4

16 small, thin sole fillets, or 8 larger ones, skinned and cut in half lengthwise
4 tbsps olive oil
1 clove garlic, crushed
Juice of ½ lemon
Finely grated rind ½ lemon
Freshly ground sea salt and black pepper, to taste
3 drops Tabasco sauce
2 medium-sized zucchini, cut into ¼ inch slices
1 green pepper, halved, seeded and cut into 1 inch pieces

1. Roll up each sole fillet like a jelly roll and secure with a wooden pick.

2. Place the fish rolls in a shallow dish. Mix together the olive oil, garlic, lemon juice, lemon rind, salt and pepper and Tabasco sauce.

3. Spoon the olive oil mixture evenly over the fish rolls, and chill for about 2 hours.

4. Remove the wooden picks, and carefully thread the rolled fish fillets onto kebab skewers alternately with the zucchini slices and pieces of green pepper.

5. Brush each threaded kebab with a little of the lemon and oil marinade.

6. Preheat the broiler. Arrange the kebab skewers on a broiler pan and place 3-5 inches from the heat for about 8 minutes, carefully turning the kebabs once or twice during cooking and brushing them with a little of the remaining marinade, if required.

TIME Preparation takes about 30 minutes, plus 2 hours chilling time, cooking takes about 8 minutes.

COOK'S TIP The marinade ingredients are delicious used with other types of fish.

MONKFISH AND PEPPER KEBABS

Monkfish is ideal for making kebabs as it can be cut into firm cubes which do not disintegrate during cooking.

SERVES 4

8 slices of bacon
1 lb monkfish, skinned and cut into 1 inch
    pieces
1 small green pepper, seeded and cut into
    1 inch pieces
1 small red pepper, seeded and cut into
    1 inch pieces
12 small mushroom caps
8 bay leaves
3 tbsps vegetable oil
½ cup dry white wine
4 tbsps tarragon vinegar
2 shallots, finely chopped
1 tbsp fresh tarragon, chopped
1 tbsp fresh chervil or parsley, chopped or
    ½ tsp dried
1 cup butter, softened
Salt and freshly ground black pepper

1. Cut the bacon slices in half lengthwise and then again in half crosswise.

2. Put a piece of the fish onto each piece of bacon and roll the bacon around the fish.

3. Thread the bacon and fish rolls onto large skewers, alternating them with pieces of pepper, the mushrooms and the bay leaves.

4. Brush the kebabs with oil and arrange on a broiler pan.

5. Preheat the broiler. Place the kebabs 3 inches from the heat and broil for 10-15 minutes, turning them frequently to prevent the kebabs from burning.

6. Heat the white wine, vinegar and shallots in a small saucepan until boiling. Cook rapidly to reduce by half.

7. Add the herbs and lower the heat.

8. Using a fork or small whisk beat the butter bit by bit into the hot wine mixture, whisking rapidly until the sauce becomes thick. Season to taste.

9. Arrange the kebabs on a serving plate and serve with a little of the sauce spooned over and the remainder in a separate jug.

TIME Preparation takes 30 minutes, cooking takes about 25 minutes.

Pizza Marinara

Seafood pizzas are wonderful – this one is especially tasty.

SERVES 4

¾ cup all-purpose flour, sifted

1 tsp baking powder

½ tsp salt

⅓ cup milk

2 tbsps salad oil

4 oz canned tomatoes

1 tsp tomato paste

1 clove crushed garlic

½ tsp dried oregano

½ tsp dried basil

Pinch of fennel seeds

Salt and pepper

¾ cup shrimp

4 anchovy fillets

8-10 mussels

1 tsp capers

2-3 black olives

4 oz sliced mozzarella cheese

1. Sift the flour, baking powder and salt into a bowl and add milk and oil. Stir vigorously until mixture leaves the sides of the bowl.

2. Press it into a ball and knead it in the bowl for about 2 minutes until smooth. Cover, and leave it to sit while preparing sauce.

3. Put the tomatoes, paste, herbs, seasoning and garlic together in a small saucepan. Bring to a boil and reduce to thicken. Leave to cool.

4. Roll out the pizza dough into a 12-inch circle. Spread the sauce evenly leaving a ½ inch border around the edge. Scatter over the shellfish, anchovy fillets, olives and capers.

5. Slice the cheese thinly and place it on top of the fish.

6. Bake in a 425°F oven for 10-15 minutes until cheese browns lightly and the crust is crisp.

TIME Preparation takes 15 minutes, cooking takes 25-30 minutes.

BROILED HERRING WITH DILL AND MUSTARD

Mustard and dill enhance the fish perfectly in this dish.

SERVES 4

---

4 tbsps fresh dill, chopped

6 tbsps mild mustard

2 tbsps lemon juice, or white wine

4-8 fresh herrings, cleaned but heads and
    tails left on

2 tbsps butter or margarine, melted

Salt and pepper

---

1. Mix the dill, mustard and lemon juice or wine together thoroughly.

2. Cut three slits, just piercing the skin, on both sides of each herring and lay them on a broiler pan.

3. Spread half the mustard mixture equally over the exposed side of each fish, pushing some into the cuts.

4. Preheat the broiler. Spoon a little of the melted butter over each herring, and broil the fish 3-5 inches from the heat for 5-6 minutes.

5. Turn the fish over and spread the remaining mustard and dill mixture over them. Spoon over the remaining melted butter and broil for another 5-6 minutes.

6. Sprinkle the fish with a little salt and pepper before serving.

TIME Preparation takes about 10 minutes, cooking takes 12-15 minutes, although this may be longer if the herring are large.

SERVING IDEAS Arrange the fish on a serving dish, garnished with lemon wedges and sprigs of fresh dill. Serve with new potatoes, if available.

TROUT IN ASPIC

A dish using crystal-clear aspic is always impressive, and home-made aspic has a flavor that is well worth the effort to make.

SERVES 4

7 cups water

2 tbsps vinegar

Pinch salt and 6 black peppercorns

2 bay leaves and 2 parsley stalks

1 small onion, diced

1¼ cups dry white wine

4 even-sized rainbow trout, cleaned and
    well washed

2 egg whites

2 level tbsps powdered gelatin

Lemon slices, capers and sprigs of fresh dill
    for garnish

1. Combine the water, vinegar, salt, peppercorns, bay leaves, parsley stalks, onion and wine in a large saucepan or fish kettle. Bring to a boil and allow to simmer for about 30 minutes.

2. Cool slightly and add the fish. Cover and bring back to simmering point. Allow the fish to cook gently for 5 minutes. Cool in the liquid, uncovered, until lukewarm.

3. Carefully remove the fish, drain and peel the skin off both sides while the fish is still slightly warm. Strain the liquid and reserve it.

4. Carefully lift the fillets from both sides of the trout, taking care not to break them up. Make sure they are completely free of skin and bones and place them on individual plates, or onto one large serving plate that has a slight well in the center.

5. Pour the reserved fish cooking liquid into a large, deep saucepan and add the egg whites. Place the pan over the heat and whisk by hand using a wire balloon whisk. Allow the mixture to come to a boil, whisking constantly. The egg whites should form a thick frothy crust on top.

6. Stop whisking and allow the liquid and egg whites to boil up the side of the pan. Take off the heat and allow to subside. Repeat the process twice more and then leave to settle.

7. Line a colander with several thicknesses of paper towels. Place in a bowl and pour the fish cooking liquid and the egg white into the colander. Leave to drain slowly. Do not allow the egg white to fall into the clarified liquid.

8. When all the liquid has drained through, remove about 1 pint and dissolve the gelatin in it. Heat again very gently if necessary to dissolve the gelatin thoroughly. Return the gelatin to the remaining stock, place the bowl in a bowl of ice water to help thicken the gelatin.

9. Decorate the trout and the bottom of the dish with lemon slices, capers and fresh dill. When the aspic has become syrupy and slightly thickened, spoon carefully over the decoration to set it. Place in the refrigerator until set.

10. The aspic may be reheated gently by placing the bowl in a pan of hot water. Do not stir the aspic too vigorously or bubbles will form. Chill again until almost set and cover the trout completely in a layer of aspic. Place in the refrigerator until completely set and serve cold.

MONKFISH IN PAPRIKA SAUCE

Monkfish is a firm, succulent fish, which should be used more often than it is. It is ideal for use in kebabs or fish casseroles, and in this recipe it is complemented magnificently by the creamy paprika sauce.

SERVES 4

1 lb monkfish fillets

Lemon juice

1 bay leaf

Slice of onion

6 peppercorns

2 tbsps butter

1 cup mushrooms, trimmed and sliced

1 small red pepper, seeded and sliced

1 shallot, finely chopped

2 tsps paprika

1 clove garlic, crushed

¼ cup all-purpose flour

1¼ cups milk

1 tbsp fresh parsley, chopped or ½ tbsp dried

1 tsp fresh thyme, chopped or ½ tsp dried

1 tsp tomato paste

Salt and pepper

8 oz fresh pasta, cooked

2 tbsps sour cream, or plain yogurt

1. Cut the monkfish into 1 inch chunks. Put these into an ovenproof dish with the lemon juice, bay leaf, onion, peppercorns and just enough water to cover. Cover with a lid and poach for about 10 minutes in a preheated oven at 350°F.

2. Melt the butter in a saucepan and stir in the mushrooms, pepper, shallot, paprika and garlic. Cook gently, until the pepper begins to soften.

3. Stir the flour into the mushrooms and pepper. Gradually add the milk, stirring until the sauce has thickened.

4. Remove the fish from the dish and strain off the liquid. Stir enough of this liquid into the sauce to make it of coating consistency. Add the parsley, thyme and tomato paste to the sauce and simmer for 2-3 minutes. Season to taste.

5. Arrange the hot, cooked pasta on a serving plate and place the fish on top. Coat with the paprika sauce, and spoon over the sour cream, or yogurt, to serve.

TIME Preparation takes about 20 minutes, and cooking takes about 16 minutes.

VARIATIONS Use any other firm-fleshed white fish instead of the monkfish.

SERVING IDEAS A mixed salad would be ideal to serve with this dish.

RED SNAPPER WITH HERB & MUSHROOM SAUCE

This fish has a slight taste of shrimp. It is often cooked with the liver left in – a delicacy.

SERVES 4

1 lb small mushrooms, left whole

1 clove garlic, finely chopped

3 tbsps olive oil

Juice of 1 lemon

1 tbsp fresh parsley, finely chopped or 1 tbsp dried

2 tsps fresh basil, finely chopped or ½ tsp dried

1 tsp fresh marjoram or sage, finely chopped or ½ tsp dried

4 tbsps dry white wine mixed with ½ tsp cornstarch

Anchovy paste

4 red snapper, each weighing about 8 oz

2 tsps white bread crumbs

2 tsps freshly grated Parmesan cheese

1. Heat the olive oil in a small frying pan and add the mushrooms and garlic. Cook over moderate heat for about 1 minute, until the garlic and mushrooms are slightly softened. Add all the herbs, lemon juice and white wine and cornstarch mixture. Bring to a boil and cook until thickened. Add anchovy essence to taste. Set aside while preparing the fish.

2. To clean the fish, cut along the stomach from the gills to the vent, the small hole near the tail. Clean out the cavity of the fish, leaving the liver, if desired.

3. To remove the gills, lift the flap and snip them out with a sharp pair of scissors. Rinse the fish well and pat dry.

4. Place the fish head to tail in a shallow ovenproof dish that can be used for serving. The fish should fit snugly into the dish.

5. Pour the prepared sauce over the fish and sprinkle with the bread crumbs and Parmesan cheese.

6. Cover the dish loosely with foil and bake in a preheated oven, 375°F, for about 20 minutes. Uncover for the last 5 minutes, if desired, and raise the oven temperature slightly. This will lightly brown the fish.

TIME Preparation takes about 30 minutes, cooking takes about 5 minutes for the sauce and 20 minutes for the fish.

COOK'S TIP If you don't want to clean the fish yourself, buy them ready-cleaned.

STUFFED SOLE

This traditional German dish is elegant enough for a formal dinner party.

SERVES 6

4 tbsps butter or margarine

2 tbsps flour

1½ cups fish or vegetable stock

1 cup button mushrooms, sliced

6 oz peeled, cooked shrimp

4 oz canned, frozen or fresh cooked
     crabmeat

4 tbsps heavy cream

2 tbsps brandy

1 oz fresh bread crumbs

Salt and pepper

6-12 sole fillets, depending upon size

4 tbsps melted butter

1. Preheat the oven to 350°F. Melt 4 tbsps butter and add the flour. Cook for about 3 minutes over gentle heat or until pale straw colored. Add the stock and bring to a boil. Add the mushrooms and allow to cook until the sauce thickens.

2. Add the cream and re-boil the sauce. Remove the sauce from the heat and add the brandy, shrimp, crab and bread crumbs.

3. Skin the sole fillets and spread the filling on the skinned side. Roll up and arrange in a buttered baking dish. Spoon melted butter over the top and cook in the pre-heated oven for 20-30 minutes, until the fish is just firm.

TIME Preparation takes about 30 minutes, cooking takes 20-30 minutes.

VARIATIONS For special occasions, substitute lobster for the crabmeat.

SERVING IDEAS Serve with a green vegetable such as broccoli, asparagus or spinach. Accompany with new potatoes tossed in parsley butter.

SARDINE AND TOMATO GRATIN

*Fresh sardines are becoming more widely available and this recipe makes the
most of these delicious fish.*

SERVES 4

3 tbsps olive oil

2 lbs large fresh sardines, descaled and
  cleaned

2 leeks, cleaned and sliced

½ cup dry white wine

6-8 tomatoes, skinned and quartered

Salt and pepper

2 tbsps fresh basil, chopped, or 1 tbsp dried
  basil

2 tbsps fresh parsley, chopped

½ cup Parmesan cheese, grated

½ cup dry bread crumbs

1. Heat the oil in a frying pan and fry the
sardines until they are brown on both sides.
It may be necessary to do this in several
batches, to prevent the fish from breaking
up.

2. When all the sardines are cooked, set
them aside and cook the leeks gently in the
sardine oil. When the leeks are soft, pour in
the wine and boil rapidly, until it is reduced
by about two thirds.

3. Add the tomatoes, seasoning and herbs
to the leeks and cook for about 1 minute.
Pour the vegetables into an ovenproof dish
and lay the sardines on top.

4. Sprinkle the cheese and bread crumbs
evenly over the sardines and bake in a
preheated oven, 425°F, for about 5 minutes.

TIME Preparation takes about 20-25 minutes, cooking takes about 15
minutes.

VARIATIONS Try substituting herrings or mackerel for the sardines. They
will take a little longer to fry.

SERVING IDEAS Cut a few anchovy fillets in half lengthwise and arrange
them in a lattice on top of the gratinée, before serving with hot garlic bread.

SWEET-SOUR FISH

In China this dish is almost always prepared with freshwater fish, but sea bass is also an excellent choice.

SERVES 2

---

1 sea bass, snapper or carp, weighing about
    2 lbs, cleaned
1 tbsp dry sherry
Few slices fresh ginger
½ cup sugar
6 tbsps cider vinegar
1 tbsp soy sauce
2 tbsps cornstarch
1 clove garlic, crushed
2 green onions, shredded
1 small carrot, peeled and finely shredded
½ cup bamboo shoots, shredded

---

1. Rinse the fish well inside and out. Make three diagonal cuts on each side of the fish with a sharp knife.

2. Trim off the fins, leaving the dorsal fin on top.

3. Trim the tail to two neat points.

4. In a wok, bring enough water to a boil to cover the fish. Gently lower the fish into the boiling water and add the sherry and ginger. Cover the wok tightly and remove at once from the heat. Allow to stand 15-20 minutes to let the fish cook in the residual heat.

5. To test if the fish is cooked, pull the dorsal fin – if it comes off easily the fish is done. If not, return the wok to the heat and bring to a boil. Remove from the heat and leave the fish to stand a further 5 minutes. Transfer the fish to a heated serving dish and keep it warm. Take all but 4 tbsps of the fish cooking liquid from the wok. Add the remaining ingredients including the vegetables and cook, stirring constantly, until the sauce thickens. Spoon some of the sauce over the fish to serve and serve the rest separately.

TIME Preparation takes about 25 minutes, cooking takes about 15-25 minutes.

COOK'S TIP The diagonal cuts in the side of the fish ensure even cooking.

SWORDFISH FLORENTINE

Swordfish has an almost "meaty" texture. Here it has a distinctly Mediterranean flavor.

SERVES 4

4 swordfish steaks, about 6-8 oz each in weight
Salt, pepper and lemon juice
Olive oil
2 lbs fresh spinach, stems removed and leaves well washed

Garlic Mayonnaise
2 egg yolks
1-2 cloves garlic
Salt, pepper and dry mustard
Pinch cayenne pepper
1 cup olive oil
Lemon juice or white wine vinegar

1. Sprinkle fish with pepper, lemon juice and olive oil. Place under a preheated broiler and broil for about 3-4 minutes per side. Fish may aso be cooked on an outdoor barbecue grill.

2. Meanwhile, use a sharp knife to shred the spinach finely. Place in a large saucepan and add a pinch of salt. Cover and cook over moderate heat with only the water that clings to the leaves after washing. Cook about 2 minutes, or until leaves are just slightly wilted. Set aside.

3. Place egg yolks in a food processor or blender. Add the garlic. Process several times to mix eggs and purée garlic. Add salt, pepper, mustard and cayenne pepper. With the machine running, pour oil through the funnel in a thin, steady stream.

4. When the sauce becomes very thick, add enough lemon juice or vinegar to thin slightly.

5. To serve, place a bed of spinach on a plate and top with the swordfish. Spoon some of the garlic mayonnaise on top of the fish and serve the rest separately.

TIME Preparation takes about 25 minutes, cooking takes about 6-8 minutes.

PREPARATION The garlic mayonnaise may be prepared in advance and will keep for 5-7 days in the refrigerator. It is also delicious served with poached shellfish, chicken or vegetables. If too thick, thin the sauce with hot water.

HALIBUT AND CRAB HOLLANDAISE

Rich and creamy, the hollandaise sauce adds an air of sophistication to this lovely dish.

SERVES 4

---

4 large fillets of halibut
1 bay leaf
Slice of onion
5 tbsps white wine
2 egg yolks
1 tbsp lemon juice
Pinch cayenne pepper
Pinch paprika
½ cup butter, melted
1 tbsp butter
2 tbsps flour
2 tbsps heavy cream
Salt and pepper
8 oz crab meat

---

1. Put the fish with the bay leaf, onion slice, wine and just enough water to cover the fish, into a baking dish. Cover and cook in a preheated oven, 325°F, for 10 minutes.

2. Put the egg yolks, lemon juice, cayenne and paprika into a blender, or food processor. Turn the machine on and gradually pour in the melted butter. Continue processing, until the hollandaise sauce is thick. Set aside.

3. Put the 1 tbsp unmelted butter into a saucepan, melt over a gentle heat and stir in the flour. Cook gently for 1 minute.

4. Remove the fish from the baking dish and strain the cooking liquid onto the flour and butter in the saucepan, stirring well to prevent lumps from forming. Cook this sauce gently, until it is smooth and has thickened. Stir in the cream, but do not allow to boil. Season to taste.

5. Stir the crab meat into the fish stock sauce and pour this mixture into a flameproof dish. Lay the halibut fillets on top and cover these with the hollandaise sauce.

6. Brown the sauce under the broiler before serving.

TIME Preparation will take about 15 minutes and cooking takes about 20 minutes.

SERVING IDEAS Serve with new potatoes and broccoli.

Trout Meunière aux Herbes

The miller (meunier) caught trout fresh from the mill stream and his wife used the flour that was on hand to dredge them with, or so the story goes.

SERVES 4

4 even-sized trout, clean and trimmed
Flour
Salt and pepper
½ cup butter
Juice of 1 lemon
2 tbsps chopped fresh herbs such as
    parsley, chervil, tarragon, thyme or
    marjoram
Lemon wedges to garnish

1. Trim the trout tails to make them more pointed. Rinse the trout well.

2. Dredge the trout with flour and shake off the excess. Season with salt and pepper. Heat half the butter in a very large frying pan and, when foaming, place in the trout. It may be necessary to cook the trout in two batches to avoid overcrowding the pan.

3. Cook over fairly high heat on both sides to brown evenly. Depending on size, the trout should take 5-8 minutes per side to cook. The dorsal fins will pull out easily when the trout are cooked. Remove the trout to a serving dish and keep them warm.

4. Wipe out the pan and add the remaining butter. Cook over moderate heat until beginning to brown, then add the lemon juice and herbs. When the lemon juice is added, the butter will bubble up and sizzle. Pour immediately over the fish and serve with lemon wedges.

TIME Preparation takes 15-20 minutes, cooking takes 5-8 minutes per side for the fish and about 5 minutes to brown the butter.

SERVING IDEAS Serve with new potatoes and peeled, cubed cucumber quickly sautéed in butter and chopped dill.

SINGAPORE FISH

The cuisine of Singapore was much influenced by that of China. In turn, the Chinese welcomed ingredients from Singapore like curry powder into their own cuisine.

SERVES 6

1 lb whitefish fillets

1 egg white

1 tbsp cornstarch

2 tsps white wine

Salt and pepper

Oil for frying

1 large onion, cut into ½ inch thick wedges

1 tbsp mild curry powder

1 small can pineapple chunks, drained and juice reserved, or ½ fresh pineapple, peeled and cubed

1 small can mandarin orange segments, drained and juice reserved

1 small can sliced water chestnuts, drained

1 tbsp cornstarch mixed with juice of 1 lime

2 tsps sugar (optional)

1. Starting at the tail end of the fillets, skin them using a sharp knife.

2. Slide the knife back and forth along the length of each fillet, pushing the fish flesh along as you go.

3. Cut the fish into even-sized pieces, about 2 inches.

4. Mix together the egg white, cornstarch, wine, salt and pepper. Place the fish in the mixture and leave to stand while heating the oil in a wok.

5. When the oil is hot, fry a few pieces of fish at a time until light golden brown and crisp. Remove the fish and put on paper towels to drain. Continue until all the fish is cooked.

6. Remove all but 1 tbsp of the oil from the wok and add the onion. Stir-fry the onion for 1-2 minutes and add the curry powder. Cook the onion and curry powder for another 1-2 minutes. Add the juice from the pineapple and mandarin oranges and bring to a boil.

7. Combine the cornstarch and lime juice and add a tablespoon of the boiling fruit juice. Return the mixture to the wok and cook until thickened, about 2 minutes. Taste and add sugar if desired. Add the fruit, water chestnuts and fried fish to the wok and stir to coat. Heat through 1 minute and serve immediately.

TIME Preparation takes about 25 minutes, cooking takes about 10 minutes.

FRIED CARP

Carp is a favorite fish in Poland and is prepared in numerous ways. This dish is popular on Christmas Eve.

SERVES 4

---

1 cleaned, scaled and filleted carp
    weighing 2-3 lbs
Salt
Flour
1-2 eggs, lightly beaten
Dry bread crumbs
Butter and oil for frying

Cabbage and Mushrooms Polish Style
16 oz canned sauerkraut
½ cup dried mushrooms
2 tbsps butter or margarine
1 onion, thinly sliced or finely chopped
1½ tbsps flour

---

1. Cut the carp into even-sized portions and sprinkle lightly with salt. Leave to stand for half an hour. Skin, if desired.

2. Place the sauerkraut in a heavy-based saucepan and add 1¼ cups water. Bring to a boil and then allow to simmer until tender.

3. Place the mushrooms in a separate pan and add enough water to cover. Cook over gentle heat until softened. Slice the mushrooms and reserve them and their cooking liquid.

4. Melt the 2 tbsps butter in a frying pan and, when foaming, add the onion. Cook in the butter until golden brown. Sprinkle over the 1½ tbsps flour and mix thoroughly.

5. When the sauerkraut is tender, strain the cooking liquid over the butter mixture. Stir very well and bring to a boil. Cook until thickened and add to the sauerkraut, along with the sliced mushrooms and their liquid. Stir thoroughly and set aside to keep warm.

6. Dredge the carp lightly with flour, shaking off the excess.

7. Coat with beaten egg using a pastry brush, or dip the pieces into the egg using two forks.

8. Coat the fish with the crumbs, shaking off the excess. Heat the butter and oil together in a large frying pan until very hot. Place in the fish and cook on both sides until golden brown – about 5 minutes per side. The oil and butter should come half way up the sides of the fish.

9. Drain fish on paper towels and serve immediately with the cabbage and mushrooms.

TIME Sauerkraut needs about 10-15 minutes to cook until tender. Fish will take about 10 minutes for both sides. It may be necessary to cook the fish in several batches, depending on the size of frying pan.

KUNG PAO SHRIMP WITH CASHEW NUTS

It is said that Kung Pao invented this dish, but to this day no one knows who he was!

SERVES 6

½ tsp fresh ginger, chopped

1 tsp garlic, chopped

1½ tbsps cornstarch

¼ tsp baking soda

Salt and pepper

¼ tsp sugar

1 lb uncooked shrimp

4 tbsps oil

1 small onion, diced

1 large or 2 small zucchini, cut into ½ inch cubes

1 small red pepper, cut into ½ inch cubes

½ cup cashew nuts

Sauce

¾ cup chicken stock

1 tbsp cornstarch

2 tsps chili sauce

2 tsps bean paste (optional)

2 tsps sesame oil

1 tbsp dry sherry or rice wine

1. Mix together the ginger, garlic, cornstarch, baking soda, salt, pepper and sugar.

2. If the shrimp are unpeeled, remove the peels and the dark vein running along the rounded side. If large, cut in half. Place in the dry ingredients and leave to stand for 20 minutes.

3. Heat the oil in a wok and when hot add the shrimp. Cook, stirring over high heat for about 20 seconds, or just until the shrimp change color. Transfer to a plate.

4. Add the onion to the same oil in the wok and cook for about 1 minute. Add the zucchini and red pepper and cook for about 30 seconds.

5. Mix the sauce ingredients together and add to the wok. Cook, stirring constantly, until the sauce is slightly thickened. Add the shrimp and the cashew nuts and heat through completely.

TIME Preparation takes about 20 minutes, cooking takes about 3 minutes.

MARINATED TROUT WITH EGG SAUCE

This recipe comes from the Navarre region of Spain, an area famous for its brook trout. The simply-prepared sauce allows the flavor of the fish to shine through.

SERVES 4

---

4 even-sized trout, cleaned but heads and
    tails left on
6 tbsps red wine
3 tbsps olive oil
3 tbsps water
1 clove garlic, crushed
2 sprigs fresh mint or pinch of dried
1 sprig fresh rosemary or pinch of dried
1 sprig fresh thyme or pinch of dried
1 small bay leaf, crumbled
6 black peppercorns
Pinch salt
3 egg yolks, lightly beaten
1 tbsp fresh mixed herbs or ½ tsp dried
Lemon or lime slices to garnish

1. Place the fish in a roasting pan and pour over the wine, oil, water and add the garlic and herbs except the 1 tbsp. Sprinkle over the peppercorns and the salt and turn the fish several times to coat them thoroughly with the marinade. Leave at room temperature for about 30 minutes.

2. Place the roasting pan with the fish on top of the stove and bring the marinade just to the simmering point. Cover the pan, place in a preheated 350°F oven and bake for about 20 minutes or until the fish is firm.

3. Transfer the fish to a serving dish and peel off the skin on one side. Cover and keep warm.

4. Strain the fish cooking liquid into a bowl or the top of a double boiler and discard any herbs and garlic left in the sieve. Mix about 3 tbsps of the liquid into the egg yolks and then return to the bowl or double boiler.

5. Heat slowly, whisking constantly until the sauce thickens. Do not allow the sauce to boil. Add the remaining herbs and adjust the seasoning.

6. Coat the sauce over the skinned side of each trout and garnish the plate with lemon or lime wedges. Serve the rest of the sauce separately.

TIME Preparation takes about 30 minutes, cooking takes about 20 minutes
for the fish and about 5 minutes to finish the sauce.

VARIATIONS The sauce may be made with white wine instead of red wine
if desired.

STUFFED FISH

A whole baked fish makes an impressive main course for a dinner party. The stuffing makes the fish go further and with no bones it's easy to serve and eat.

SERVES 4-6

2-3 lb whole fish such as carp or sea bass
Salt and pepper
2 tbsps melted butter

Stuffing

1 tbsp butter or margarine
1 small onion, finely chopped
1½ cups mushrooms, coarsely chopped
1 hard-cooked egg, peeled and coarsely
    chopped
¾ cup fresh bread crumbs, white or whole-
    wheat
Pinch salt and pepper
2 tsps fresh dill, chopped
2 tsps fresh parsley, chopped
Pinch nutmeg

Sauce

½ cup sour cream
Pinch sugar
Grated rind and juice of ½ lemon
Pinch salt and white pepper
Lemon slices and parsley sprigs to garnish

1. Ask the assistant to gut and bone the fish for you, leaving on the head and tail. Sprinkle the cavity of the fish with salt and pepper and set it aside while preparing the stuffing.

2. To chop the onion finely, peel it and cut it in half lengthwise. Place the onion cut side down on a chopping board. Using a large, sharp knife, make four cuts into the onion, parallel to the chopping board, but not completely through to the root end. Using the pointed tip of the knife, make four or five cuts into the onion lengthwise, following the natural lines in the onion and not cutting through to the root end. Next, cut the onion crosswise into thin or thick slices as desired and the onion should fall apart into individual dice. Keep fingers well out of the way when slicing.

3. Melt the butter or margarine in a medium-sized saucepan and add the chopped onion and mushrooms. Cook briefly to soften the vegetables and take off the heat. Stir in the remaining stuffing ingredients.

4. Spread the stuffing evenly into the cavity of the fish, sprinkle the top with melted butter and place the fish in lightly buttered foil in a large baking dish. Bake in a preheated 350°F oven for about 40 minutes, basting frequently.

5. When the fish is cooked, combine the sauce ingredients and pour over the fish. Cook another 5 minutes to heat the sauce, but do not allow it to bubble. Remove the fish to a serving dish and garnish with lemon and parsley.

TIME Preparation takes about 20 minutes. If boning the fish yourself, add a further 30 minutes. Cooking takes approximately 45 minutes.

COOK'S TIP Cover the head and tail of the fish with lightly greased foil about halfway through cooking time. This will prevent the fish from drying out and improve the appearance of the finished dish.

PAELLA

This dish has as many variations as Spain has cooks! Fish, meat and poultry combine with vegetables and rice to make a complete meal.

SERVES 6

12 mussels in their shells

6 clams

Flour

6 oz cod, skinned and cut into 2 inch pieces

12 large shrimp

3 chorizos or other spicy sausage

3 tbsps oil

2 lb chicken, cut in 12 serving-size pieces

1 small onion, chopped

1 clove garlic, crushed

2 small peppers, red and green, seeded and shredded

3 cups long grain rice

Large pinch saffron

Salt and pepper

4 cups boiling water

4 oz frozen peas

3 tomatoes, peeled, seeded and chopped or shredded

1. Scrub the clams and mussels well to remove beards and barnacles. Discard any with broken shells or those that do not close when tapped. Leave the mussels and clams to soak in water with a handful of flour for 30 minutes.

2. Remove the heads and legs from the shrimp, if desired, but leave on the tail shells.

3. Place the sausage in a saucepan and cover with water. Bring to a boil and then simmer for 5 minutes. Drain and slice into ¼ inch rounds. Set aside.

4. Heat the oil and fry the chicken pieces, browning evenly on both sides. Remove and drain on paper towels.

5. Add the sausage, onions, garlic and peppers to the oil in the frying pan and fry briskly for about 3 minutes.

6. Combine the sausage mixture with uncooked rice and saffron and place in a special paella dish or a large oven- and flame-proof casserole. Pour on the water, season with salt and pepper and bring to a boil. Stir occasionally and allow to boil for about 2 minutes.

7. Add the chicken pieces and place in a preheated 400°F oven for about 15 minutes.

8. Add the clams, mussels, shrimp, cod and peas and bake another 10-15 minutes or until the rice is tender, chicken is cooked and mussels and clams open. Discard any that do not open. Add the tomatoes 5 minutes before the end of cooking time and serve immediately.

TIME Preparation takes about 30-40 minutes, cooking takes about 35-40 minutes.

SOLE WITH SPICY TOMATO SAUCE

This delicious recipe mixes white fish with a spicy Mexican sauce.

SERVES 4

---

3 oz cream cheese
1 tsp dried oregano
Pinch cayenne pepper
4 whole fillets of sole
Lime slices and dill to garnish

Tomato Sauce
1 tbsp oil
1 small onion, chopped
1 celery stalk, chopped
1 chili pepper, seeded and chopped
¼ tsp each ground cumin, coriander and
    ginger
½ red and ½ green pepper, seeded and
    chopped
14 oz can tomatoes
1 tbsp tomato paste
Salt, pepper and a pinch sugar

---

1. Heat the oil in a heavy-based pan and cook the onion, celery, chili pepper and spices for about 5 minutes over very low heat.

2. Add red and green peppers and the remaining ingredients and bring to a boil. Reduce heat and simmer for 15-20 minutes, stirring occasionally. Set aside while preparing the fish.

3. Mix the cream cheese, oregano and cayenne pepper together and set aside.

4. Skin the fillets using a filleting knife. Start at the tail end and hold the knife at a slight angle to the skin.

5. Push the knife along using a sawing motion, with the blade against the skin. Dip fingers in salt to make it easier to hold onto the fish skin. Gradually separate the fish from the skin.

6. Spread the cheese filling on all 4 fillets and roll each up. Secure with wooden picks.

7. Place the fillets in a lightly greased baking dish, cover and bake for 10 minutes in a preheated 350°F oven.

8. Pour over the tomato sauce and bake another 10-15 minutes. Fish is cooked when it feels firm and looks opaque. Garnish with lime slices and dill.

TIME Preparation takes about 30 minutes and cooking takes 20-25 minutes.

SERVING IDEAS Add rice and an avocado salad.

Smoked Haddock and Egg Quiche

This classic quiche is a firm favorite for lunches and suppers alike.

SERVES 6

8 oz ready-made whole-wheat dough
12 oz smoked haddock fillet
½ cup chicken stock
2 hard-cooked eggs, chopped
1 tbsp fresh chives, chopped
¾ cup Cheddar cheese, grated
3 eggs
1 cup milk
Salt and pepper

1. Roll out the pastry to fit a 9 inch deep fluted pie pan. Press the edges up well and push the base well down. Prick the base with a fork and bake for 15 minutes in a preheated oven, 375°F.

2. Place the fish in a saucepan and poach gently in the chicken stock for about 8 minutes, or until just tender. Drain the fish and flake it into a bowl, discarding any skin or bones.

3. Mix the chopped eggs, chives and cheese into the fish, and spread this mixture evenly into the part-baked pastry shell.

4. Beat together the eggs and milk, and season to taste. Pour over the fish mixture in the pastry shell.

5. Bake at 375°F for 25-30 minutes, or until the filling is set.

TIME Preparation will take about 25 minutes, and cooking takes about 40 minutes.

CHILLED FISH CURRY

This sophisticated, mild curry will serve four as a refreshing summer lunch, or eight as an elegant appetizer.

SERVES 4-8

8 oz fresh salmon fillet
12 oz whitefish fillet
Chicken stock
Salt and pepper
½ cup mayonnaise
1½ cups plain yogurt
2 tsps curry powder
Juice and grated rind of ½ lemon
¾ cup peeled shrimp

Garnish
Kiwi fruit, peeled and sliced
Sprigs fresh mint
Shredded coconut

1. Put the salmon and whitefish fillets into a shallow pan and add just enough chicken stock to cover.

2. Season to taste and simmer gently, until the fish is just tender.

3. Remove the fish carefully from the cooking liquid and leave to cool slightly.

4. In a medium-sized bowl, mix together the mayonnaise and the yogurt. Blend in the curry powder and the lemon juice and rind.

5. Flake the cooked fish, removing any bones and skin. Mix the flaked fish and the shrimp into the curry sauce.

6. Arrange the fish curry on serving plates and garnish with slices of kiwi fruit, sprigs of fresh mint and coconut.

TIME Preparation takes about 20 minutes, and cooking takes about 6 minutes.

VARIATIONS If you prefer, use slices of peeled cucumber instead of the kiwi fruit.

Rainbow Trout with Spinach and Walnut Stuffing

SERVES 6-8

1 fresh whole rainbow trout, weighing
   2½ lbs, cleaned and boned
2 lbs fresh spinach
1 small onion
¼ cup polyunsaturated margarine
⅓ cup walnuts, coarsely chopped
4 oz fresh white bread crumbs
1 tbsp fresh parsley, chopped or ½ tsp dried
1 tbsp fresh thyme, chopped or ½ tsp dried
¼ grated nutmeg
Salt and freshly ground black pepper
Juice of 2 lemons
Watercress sprigs and lemon slices, to garnish

1. If you cannot buy the fish boned, remove the bone yourself. Carefully cut the underside of the fish from the end of the slit made when the fish was cleaned, to the tip of the tail.

2. Place the fish, belly side down, on a flat work surface, spreading the cut underside out to balance the fish more easily.

3. Using the palm of your hand press down along the backbone of the fish, pushing the spine downwards towards the work surface.

4. Turn the fish over and using a sharp knife, carefully pull the backbone away from the fish, cutting it away with scissors at the base of the head and tail.

5. Remove the backbone completely and pull out any loose bones you may find with a pair of tweezers. Lay the boned fish in the center of a large square of lightly oiled aluminum foil and set aside.

6. Wash the spinach leaves well and tear off any coarse stalks. Put the spinach into a large saucepan and sprinkle with salt. Do not add any extra water. Cover and cook over a moderate heat for about 3 minutes.

7. Turn the spinach into a colander and drain well, pressing with the back of a wooden spoon to remove all the excess moisture.

8. Chop the cooked spinach very finely using a sharp knife.

9. Peel and chop the onion finely and fry gently in about 1 tbsp of the margarine until soft, but not colored.

10. Stir the cooked onion into the chopped spinach along with the walnuts, bread crumbs, herbs, nutmeg, salt, pepper and half of the lemon juice. Mix well to blend evenly.

11. Use the spinach stuffing to fill the cavity inside the trout. Push the stuffing in firmly, re-shaping the fish as you do so. Allow a little of the stuffing to show between the cut edge of the fish.

12. Seal the foil over the top of the fish, but do not wrap it too tightly.

13. Place the fish in a roasting pan and bake in a preheated oven at 350°F for 35 minutes.

14. Carefully unwrap the fish and transfer it to a large serving dish.

15. Using a sharp knife, peel away the skin from all exposed sides of the fish. If possible remove some skin from the underside also.

16. While the fish is still hot, dot with the remaining margarine, sprinkle with the remaining lemon juice, then serve garnished with the watercress and sliced lemon.

TIME Preparation takes 35-40 minutes, cooking takes about 40 minutes.

SZECHUAN FISH

The piquant spiciness of Szechuan pepper is quite different from that of black or white pepper. Beware, though, too much can numb the mouth temporarily!

SERVES 6

Whole chili peppers
1 lb whitefish fillets
Pinch salt and pepper
1 egg
5 tbsps flour
6 tbsps white wine
Flour for dredging
Oil for frying
2 oz cooked ham, cut in small dice
1 inch piece fresh ginger, finely diced
½-1 red or green chili pepper, cored,
    seeded and finely diced
6 water chestnuts, finely diced
4 green onions, finely chopped
3 tbsps light soy sauce
1 tsp cider vinegar or rice wine vinegar
½ tsp ground Szechuan pepper (optional)
1¼ cups light fish stock
1 tbsp cornstarch dissolved with 2 tbsps
    water
2 tsps sugar

1. To prepare the garnish, choose unblemished chili peppers with the stems on. Using a small, sharp knife, cut the peppers in strips, starting from the pointed end.

2. Cut down to within ½ inch of the stem end. Rinse out the seeds under cold running water and place the peppers in iced water.

3. Leave the peppers to soak for at least 4 hours or overnight until they open up like flowers.

4. Cut the fish fillets into 2 inch pieces and season with salt and pepper. Beat the egg well and add flour and wine to make a batter. Dredge the fish lightly with flour and then dip into the batter. Mix the fish well.

5. Heat a wok and when hot, add enough oil to deep-fry the fish. When the oil is hot, fry a few pieces of fish at a time, until golden brown. Drain and proceed until all the fish is cooked.

6. Remove all but 1 tbsp of oil from the wok and add the ham, ginger, diced chili pepper, water chestnuts and green onions. Cook for about 1 minute and add the soy sauce and vinegar. If using Szechuan pepper, add at this point. Stir well and cook for another 1 minute. Remove the vegetables from the pan and set them aside.

7. Add the stock to the wok and bring to a boil. When boiling, add 1 spoonful of the hot stock to the cornstarch mixture. Add the mixture back to the stock and reboil, stirring constantly until thickened.

8. Stir in the sugar and return the fish and vegetables to the sauce. Heat through for 30 seconds and serve at once.

TIME Preparation takes about 30 minutes. Chili pepper garnish takes at least 4 hours to soak. Cooking takes about 10 minutes.

FISH MILANESE

These fish, cooked in the style of Milan, have a crispy crumb coating and the fresh tang of lemon juice.

SERVES 4

---

8 sole fillets
2 tbsps dry vermouth
1 bay leaf
6 tbsps olive oil
Seasoned flour for dredging
2 eggs, lightly beaten
Dry bread crumbs
Oil for shallow frying
6 tbsps butter
1 clove garlic, crushed
2 tsps parsley, chopped
2 tbsps capers
1 tsp fresh oregano, chopped
Juice of 1 lemon
Lemon wedges and parsley to garnish

1. Skin the fillets with a sharp filleting knife. Remove any small bones and place the fillets in a large, shallow dish. Combine the vermouth, oil and bay leaf in a small saucepan and heat gently. Allow to cool completely and pour over the fish. Leave the fish to marinate for about 1 hour turning them occasionally.

2. Remove the fish from the marinade and dredge lightly with the seasoned flour.

3. Dip the fillets into the beaten eggs to coat, or use a pastry brush to brush the eggs onto the fillets. Dip the egg-coated fillet into the bread crumbs, pressing the crumbs on firmly.

4. Heat the oil in a large frying pan. Add the fillets and cook slowly, about 3 minutes, on both sides until golden brown. Remove and drain on paper towels.

5. Pour the oil out of the frying pan and wipe it clean. Add the butter and the garlic and cook until both turn a light brown. Add the herbs, capers and lemon juice and pour immediately over the fish. Garnish with lemon wedges and sprigs of parsley.

TIME Preparation takes 1 hour for the fish to marinate, cooking takes about 6 minutes. It may be necessary to cook the fish in several batches, depending upon the size of the frying pan.

HERRING WITH APPLES

The addition of fresh tasting apples beautifully complements the delicious and wholesome flavor of herring.

SERVES 4

---

4 herrings, cleaned
2 large apples
1 large onion, peeled and thinly sliced
4 large potatoes, peeled and sliced
Salt and freshly ground black pepper
½ cup apple cider
2 oz dried bread crumbs
¼ cup polyunsaturated margarine
1 tbsp fresh parsley, chopped

---

1. Cut the heads and tails from the herrings and split them open from the underside.

2. Put the herring, belly side down, on a flat surface and carefully press along the back of each fish with the palm of your hand, pushing the backbone down towards the surface.

3. Turn the herring over and with a sharp knife, carefully prise away the backbone, pulling out any loose bones as you go. Do not cut the fish into separate fillets. Wash and dry them well.

4. Peel, quarter, core and slice one of the apples.

5. Lightly grease a shallow baking pan and layer with the potatoes, apple and onions, seasoning well with salt and pepper between layers.

6. Pour the apple cider over the layers and cover the dish with foil. Bake in a preheated oven 350°F for 40 minutes.

7. Remove the dish from the oven and arrange the herring fillets over the top.

8. Sprinkle the bread crumbs over the herrings and dot with half of the margarine.

9. Increase the oven temperature to 400°F and return the dish to the oven for about 10-15 minutes, or until the herrings are cooked and brown.

10. Core the remaining apple and slice into rounds, leaving the peel on.

11. Melt the remaining margarine in a frying pan and gently fry the apple slices.

12. Remove the herrings from the oven and garnish with the fried apple slices and chopped parsley. Serve at once.

TIME Preparation takes 15-20 minutes, cooking takes about 50 minutes.

COOK'S TIP If you do not want to bone the fish yourself, buy boned fish.

SEA BASS WITH VEGETABLES

A delicious lemon sauce perfectly enhances the fish in this impressive dish.

SERVES 4

1 sea bass, weighing 2-2½ lbs
8 oz broccoli or green beans
1 lb new potatoes
4 zucchini
4 very small turnips
1 small bunch green onions
2 carrots
¼ cup butter
¼ cup flour
1¼ cups milk
1 small bunch fresh thyme or 1 tbsp dried
3 lemons
Paprika
Fresh parsley, chopped
Salt and pepper

1. Clean the bass, trim the fins, but leave the head and tail on. Put salt and pepper and half thyme inside the fish. Put the fish in the center of a large square of buttered foil. Add the juice of 1 lemon, wrap fish loosely, and bake at 350°F for 40-60 minutes, depending on weight.

2. Cut the broccoli into small florets (or trim the beans, but leave whole). Scrub potatoes and turnips but do not peel. Cut the zucchini into 2-inch strips. Trim the green onions, leaving some of the green. Peel the carrots, and cut to the same size as the zucchini.

3. Keeping the vegetables in separate piles, steam the potatoes and turnips for 15-20 minutes, the carrots, broccoli or beans for 6 minutes, and the zucchini and green onions for 3 minutes. Arrange on a serving dish and keep warm.

4. Remove the fish from its wrapping and place in the middle of the vegetables; keep them warm while preparing the sauce.

5. Melt the butter, add the flour and cook gently for 1-2 minutes until pale brown. Stir in the milk, add the flour gradually, stirring constantly. Bring the sauce to boil for 1-2 minutes until thick. Strain in the cooking liquid from the fish.

6. Peel and segment the remaining lemons, working over a bowl to collect any juice. Chop the remaining thyme and add to the sauce along with lemon segments and juice.

7. Sprinkle paprika on the potatoes, and chopped parsley on the carrots. Coat the fish with lemon sauce and serve.

TIME Preparation takes 30 minutes, cooking takes 40-60 minutes.

Index

Photography by Peter Barry
Recipes styled by Helen Burdett
Recipes by Judith Ferguson
Designed by Richard Hawke